CW00405919

AI Unplug
Comprehensive Guide to
Understanding and Working
with Artificial Intelligence

electronic means or printed format. Recording this publication is strictly prohibited, and any storage of this document is not allowed unless with written permission from the publisher. All rights reserved.

The information provided herein is stated to be truthful and consistent in that any liability, in terms of inattention or otherwise, by any usage or abuse of any policies, processes, or directions contained within is the solitary and utter responsibility of the recipient reader. Under no circumstances will any legal responsibility or blame be held against the publisher for any reparation, damages, or monetary loss due to the information herein, either directly or indirectly.

Want to receive exclusive updates, promotions, and bonus content related to this book and others, plus the chance to win free books? Look no further! Simply scan the QR code above and enter your email address on the landing page to join our email list.

As a member of our email list, you'll receive:

- Insider information and behind-the-scenes insights

- Special promotions and discounts on future purchases
- Early notification of future book releases
- The chance to win free books through our monthly sweepstakes

Don't wait - scan the QR code and join our email list today for your chance to win!

Table of content

Chapter 1: Introduction to Artificial Intelligence

Have you ever wondered what it would be like to have a personal assistant that could anticipate your needs, answer your questions, and perform tasks on your behalf? Or have you imagined a world in which self-driving cars are the norm and traffic accidents are a thing of the past? These scenarios may seem like science fiction, but they are rapidly becoming a reality thanks to advances in artificial intelligence (AI).

But what exactly is AI, and how does it work? In its simplest form, AI refers to the ability of a machine or computer system to perform tasks that would normally require human intelligence, such as learning, problem-solving, and decision-making. While the concept of AI has been around for centuries, it was not until the development of the computer in the 20th century that it became possible to build machines with the capacity to process and analyse large amounts of data, paving the way for the modern field of AI.

One of the most significant milestones in the history of AI occurred in 1997 when a computer program called Deep Blue defeated world champion chess player Garry Kasparov in a highly publicised match. Developed by IBM, Deep Blue was the first computer to defeat a human world champion at chess, and its success marked a major step forward for AI research and development (Campbell, 2002).

Since the development of Deep Blue, AI has made tremendous progress, with advances in areas such as machine learning, natural language processing, and robotics. Today, AI is used in a wide range of applications, from self-driving cars and personal assistants to medical diagnosis and financial forecasting.

But as AI continues to evolve and become more integrated into our daily lives, it raises a number of important questions and ethical considerations. How will AI impact the job market and economy? What are the potential risks and unintended consequences of using AI, and how can we mitigate them? And what is the potential for superintelligent AI, and what might be the implications for humanity?

To understand these questions and the broader context of AI, it is important to explore the history and evolution of the field. The concept of artificial intelligence has a long and varied history, with roots dating back to ancient Greece and the myth of Pygmalion, a sculptor who created a statue of a woman that came to life. In the modern era, the first recorded use of the term "artificial intelligence" was in a proposal for a conference on the subject by John McCarthy, a computer scientist and cognitive scientist, in 1955 (Bostrom, 2014).

Since then, AI has undergone several major stages of development. In the 1950s and 1960s, the focus was on creating programs that could perform specific tasks, such as playing chess or solving mathematical problems. This type of AI, known as narrow or "weak" AI, is specialised and limited to a specific domain.

In the 1980s and 1990s, researchers began to develop more general-purpose AI systems capable of learning and adapting to new situations. This type of AI, known as general or "strong" AI, is designed to be more flexible and adaptable and is capable of performing a wide range of tasks.

More recently, there has been growing interest in the development of superintelligent AI, which is characterised by intelligence that surpasses that of any human. While the potential benefits of superintelligent AI are significant, there are also concerns about the risks and unintended consequences of creating a machine that is more intelligent than its creators (Bostrom, 2014).

Today, AI is used in a wide range of applications, from self-driving cars and personal assistants to medical diagnosis and financial forecasting. In the following sections, we will explore the different types and applications of AI in more detail, as well as the ethical and societal implications of this rapidly evolving field. We will also provide tips and strategies for working with AI in a responsible and effective manner, and consider the potential impacts of AI on various industries and sectors.

Chapter 2: The Science of Artificial Intelligence

One of the key features that sets artificial intelligence (AI) apart from other technologies is its ability to learn and adapt. Through the use of machine learning algorithms and neural networks, AI systems can analyse data, identify patterns, and make decisions based on those patterns without being explicitly programmed to do so.

Machine learning is a subset of AI that involves the use of algorithms to automatically learn from data and improve performance over time. There are several different types of machine learning, including supervised learning, unsupervised learning, and reinforcement learning.

In supervised learning, the AI system is provided with labelled training data, which includes both input data and the corresponding correct output. For example, if the AI system is being trained to recognise images of animals, the training data might include thousands of images of animals labelled with their species (e.g., "cat," "dog," "bird," etc.). The AI system uses this labelled data to learn how to classify new images based on the patterns and features it has identified in the training data.

Unsupervised learning involves the use of algorithms to identify patterns in data without being provided with labelled examples. This type of machine learning is often used for anomaly detection or clustering, in which the AI system groups data points into clusters based on common characteristics.

Reinforcement learning involves the use of rewards and punishments to teach the AI system to make decisions that maximise a specific goal or objective. For example, a self-driving car might be programmed to prioritise safety over speed and would be "rewarded" for making safe decisions and "punished" for making risky decisions.

In addition to machine learning, AI systems often rely on neural networks, which are computer systems modelled after the structure and function of the human brain. Neural networks consist of layers of interconnected nodes, or "neurons," which process and transmit information. The connections between neurons are weighted, meaning that some Connections are stronger or more important than others, and the weights can be adjusted based on the data the neural network is processing.

Neural networks are particularly useful for tasks that involve pattern recognition or image classification, such as image recognition or natural language processing. They are also used in robotics for tasks such as object recognition or motion planning.

In the following sections, we will explore the various technologies and approaches used in AI in more detail, including machine learning and neural networks. We will also provide case studies and examples of AI in action to help illustrate the capabilities and potential of this exciting field.

Case Studies and Examples of AI in Action

One of the most exciting aspects of artificial intelligence (AI) is its potential to transform a wide range of industries and sectors, from healthcare and transportation to education and entertainment. In this section, we will explore a few examples of how AI is being used in practice to give a sense of the diverse applications and possibilities of this technology.

Healthcare: In the healthcare industry, AI is being used to assist with a variety of tasks, from diagnosing diseases and predicting patient outcomes to identifying potential outbreaks of infectious diseases. For example, a study published in the Journal of the American Medical Association (JAMA) found that an AI system was able to accurately diagnose skin cancer with the same accuracy as human dermatologists (Esteva et al., 2017). AI is also being used to analyse electronic health records and identify patterns that could help predict patient outcomes and guide treatment decisions (Doshi et al., 2016).

Transportation: AI is also playing a significant role in the transportation industry with the development of self-driving cars and intelligent transportation systems. Self-driving cars use a combination of sensors, cameras, and machine learning algorithms to navigate roads and avoid obstacles, with the goal of reducing accidents and improving traffic flow. Intelligent transportation systems use sensors and AI to monitor traffic conditions and optimise the movement of vehicles and pedestrians, for example, by adjusting traffic signals or routing traffic around accidents or bottlenecks (Gao et al., 2017).

Education: AI is also being used in the education sector to personalise learning and improve student outcomes. For example, adaptive learning platforms use AI to assess a student's current knowledge and skill level and provide customised learning materials and assignments based on the student's needs and goals (Baldwin et al., 2016). AI is also being used to grade essays and other written assignments, allowing teachers to spend more time providing feedback and support to students (Gabelica et al., 2016).

Entertainment: In the entertainment industry, AI is being used to create new types of content and experiences. For example, AI-generated music and art are becoming increasingly sophisticated and are being used in a variety of contexts, from film scores and video game soundtracks to museum exhibits (Hogenboom, 2016). AI is also being used to create personalised content recommendations and to improve the user experience in video streaming platforms and other digital media outlets (Guo et al., 2018).

These are just a few examples of the many ways in which AI is being used in practice. As the field continues to evolve and advance, it is likely that we will see even more innovative and transformative applications of AI in the future.

Conclusion

In this chapter, we have explored the science behind artificial intelligence (AI), including the key technologies and approaches used in the field. We have also provided case studies and examples of AI in action to give a sense of the diverse applications and possibilities of this exciting technology.

In the next chapter, we will turn our attention to the future of AI and consider the potential impacts of this technology on the job market and economy, as well as the risks and unintended consequences of using AI. We will also explore the potential for superintelligent AI and its implications for humanity and consider the ethical considerations and guidelines for responsible AI development and use.

References

Baldwin, A., et al. (2016). Personalised learning with adaptive instruction: A review of research on its effectiveness. Review of Educational Research, 86(2), 435-481.

Bostrom, N. (2014). Superintelligence: Paths, dangers, and strategies. Oxford, UK: Oxford University Press.

Campbell, M. (2002). Deep blue: An artificial intelligence milestone. Communications of the ACM, 45(6), 57-61.

Doshi, P., et al. (2016). The potential for artificial intelligence in healthcare: A review.

Journal of the American Medical Association, 316(22), 2426-2436.

Esteva, A., et al. (2017). Dermatologist-level classification of skin cancer with deep neural networks. Nature, 542(7639), 115-118.

Gabelica, V., et al. (2016). Automated essay scoring: A review. Educational Psychology Review, 28(4), 661-680.

Gao, Y., et al. (2017). Intelligent transportation systems: A review. Transportation Research Part C: Emerging Technologies, 78, 1-18.

Guo, Y., et al. (2018). Personalised content recommendation using artificial intelligence techniques: A review. ACM Computing Surveys, 51(1), 1-36.

Hogenboom, M. (2016). How artificial intelligence is revolutionising the arts. BBC News. Retrieved from https://www.bbc.com/news/entertainment-arts-36656741.

In this chapter, we have provided an overview of the science behind artificial intelligence (AI), including the key technologies and approaches used in the field. We have also explored a few examples of how AI is being used in practice in a variety of sectors and industries. In the next chapter, we will consider the potential impacts of AI on the job market and economy, as well as the risks and unintended consequences of using this technology. We will also explore the potential for superintelligent AI and its implications for humanity and consider the ethical considerations and guidelines for responsible AI development and use.

Chapter 3: The Future of Artificial Intelligence

One of the most exciting aspects of artificial intelligence (AI) is its potential to shape the future of work, society, and humanity. In this chapter, we will consider the potential impacts of AI on the job market and economy, as well as the risks and unintended consequences of using this technology. We will also explore the potential for superintelligent AI and its implications for humanity and consider the ethical considerations and guidelines for responsible AI development and use.

Impacts of AI on the Job Market and Economy

There is no doubt that AI has the potential to revolutionize the job market and economy, by automating tasks and processes that are currently performed by humans. According to a report by the World Economic Forum (WEF), more than 75 million jobs may be displaced by AI and automation by 2025, while 133 million new jobs may be created (WEF, 2018). This represents a net gain of 58 million jobs, but the nature of these jobs is likely to be significantly different from those that are being replaced.

For example, jobs that involve repetitive tasks or that can be easily automated are more likely to be displaced by AI, while jobs that require human interaction or creativity are less likely to be automated (Frey & Osborne, 2013). This could lead to significant shifts in the job market, as workers need to adapt to new roles and industries.

The impact of AI on the economy is also likely to be significant as businesses and organisations adopt AI to increase efficiency and reduce costs. According to a study by McKinsey & Company, AI has the potential to contribute an additional $13 trillion to the global economy by 2030 through increased productivity and consumer surplus (McKinsey Global Institute, 2018). However, this potential gain is not evenly distributed, and some sectors and regions may benefit more than others.

Risks and Unintended Consequences of Using AI

While AI has the potential to bring many benefits, it also carries risks and unintended consequences that need to be carefully managed. One of the main risks of AI is the possibility of biased or unfair decision-making. AI systems are only as fair and unbiased as the data they are trained on, and if the data is biased, the AI system will be as well. This can lead to discriminatory outcomes, such as the algorithm used by a major US credit scoring company that was found to discriminate against African Americans and Hispanics (Angwin et al., 2016).

Another risk of AI is the possibility of unintended consequences, as AI systems may make decisions that are unexpected or unintended by their designers. For example, an AI system designed to optimise traffic flow might route cars through a residential neighbourhood to avoid a traffic jam on a major road, causing disruption and inconvenience for the residents (Chen et al., 2017).

There is also a risk of hacking or misuse of AI systems, as AI is vulnerable to the same types of cyber attacks as other computer systems. For example, a self-driving car could be hacked and forced to drive off the road or into oncoming traffic (Gao et al., 2018).

Potential for Superintelligent AI and Its Implications for Humanity

One of the most controversial and debated topics in the field of AI is the potential for superintelligent AI, or AI that is significantly more intelligent than human beings. Some experts believe that it is only a matter of time before we develop AI that surpasses human intelligence in a wide range of domains and that this could have profound implications for humanity (Bostrom, 2014).

While the potential for superintelligent AI is still largely speculative, there are a few scenarios that are often discussed in the literature. One possibility is that superintelligent AI could be used to solve some of humanity's most pressing problems, such as disease, poverty, and environmental degradation

(Bostrom, 2014). Superintelligent AI could also be used to create new technologies and innovations that are beyond the capabilities of human beings, leading to exponential economic growth and prosperity (McKinsey Global Institute, 2018).

However, there are also potential risks and downsides to the development of superintelligent AI. For example, there is a risk that superintelligent AI could be used for malicious purposes, such as warfare or espionage (Bostrom, 2014). There is also a risk that superintelligent AI could become uncontrollable or unmanageable, leading to unintended consequences that are difficult or impossible to reverse (Bostrom, 2014).

Finally, there is a risk that superintelligent AI could pose a threat to human beings themselves, either by surpassing us in intelligence and taking over the world or by becoming indifferent or hostile to our needs and values (Bostrom, 2014). While these scenarios are highly speculative and unlikely, they highlight the need for careful consideration and ethical guidelines for the development and use of superintelligent AI.

Ethical Considerations and Guidelines for Responsible AI Development and Use

Given the potential risks and unintended consequences of AI, it is important to consider the ethical considerations and guidelines for responsible AI development and use. There are a number of organisations and initiatives that are working on developing ethical guidelines for AI, including the IEEE Global Initiative on Ethics of Autonomous and Intelligent Systems, the Association for Computing Machinery (ACM) Code of Ethics, and the European Union's High-Level Expert Group on Artificial Intelligence.

These guidelines generally recommend a number of principles for responsible AI development and use, such as transparency, accountability, fairness, and respect for human rights. For example, the ACM Code of Ethics recommends that AI developers "be honest and trustworthy," "respect privacy," and "consider

the potential consequences of their work"
(ACM, 1992).

Conclusion

In this chapter, we have considered the potential impacts of artificial intelligence (AI) on the job market and economy, as well as the risks and unintended consequences of using this technology. We have also explored the potential for superintelligent AI and its implications for humanity and considered the ethical considerations and guidelines for responsible AI development and use.

In the next chapter, we will turn our attention to the current state of AI development and deployment and explore the major players and trends in the field. We will also consider the role of government and regulation in shaping the direction and trajectory of AI, and the role of civil society in advocating for responsible and ethical AI development and use.

Chapter 4: Working with Artificial Intelligence

As artificial intelligence (AI) becomes increasingly prevalent in our society, more and more organizations and individuals are looking to incorporate this powerful technology into their operations and activities. However, working with AI can be challenging, as it requires a different set of skills, knowledge, and strategies than working with traditional systems and technologies.

In this chapter, we will explore tips and strategies for successfully incorporating AI into your organization or personal life. We will look at best practices for managing and collaborating with AI systems, and provide case studies and examples of successful AI implementation.

One of the key considerations when working with AI is understanding the capabilities and limitations of the technology. AI systems are designed to perform specific tasks and make decisions based on the data and algorithms that they have been trained on. Therefore, it is important to have a clear understanding of the capabilities and limitations of the specific AI system that you are working with.

Another important aspect of working with AI is developing the right team and infrastructure to support your AI initiatives. This may include hiring experts in AI, data science, and machine learning, as well as creating dedicated teams or departments to manage and maintain your AI systems.

Once you have the right team and infrastructure in place, it is important to establish clear goals and objectives for your AI initiatives. This may include identifying specific business problems that you hope to solve with AI, or developing a strategy for using AI to gain a competitive advantage.

It's also crucial to have a clear plan for managing and collaborating with your AI systems. This may include developing guidelines and protocols for working with the systems, as well as establishing communication and feedback mechanisms to ensure that the systems are performing as expected.

One of the best ways to learn about working with AI is by studying real-world examples and case studies of successful AI implementation. In this chapter, we will provide case studies of organizations and individuals who have successfully incorporated AI into their operations, and explore the strategies and best practices that they used to achieve success.

By understanding the tips and strategies for successfully incorporating AI into your organization or personal life, as well as best practices for managing and collaborating with AI systems, you will be well-prepared to take advantage of the many benefits that this powerful technology has to offer.

Additionally, it is important to consider the ethical and societal implications of AI, as it has the potential to disrupt various industries and displace jobs. It is vital to ensure that the development and use of AI aligns with values such as fairness, accountability and transparency to prevent negative impacts on society.

Another important aspect to consider is the potential for bias in AI systems, as they are only as unbiased as the data they are trained on. Therefore, it is crucial to ensure that the data used to train AI systems is diverse and representative, and to actively monitor and address any potential biases in the system's decision-making.

In summary, working with AI requires a multifaceted approach and careful consideration of various factors. By understanding the capabilities and limitations of AI, developing the right team and infrastructure, setting clear goals, establishing best practices for managing and collaborating with AI systems, considering the ethical and societal implications, and studying real-world examples, organizations and individuals can successfully incorporate AI into their operations.

Chapter 5: The Ethical Implications of Artificial Intelligence

As artificial intelligence (AI) becomes more advanced and integrated into our society, it is important to consider the ethical implications of this powerful technology. From concerns about job displacement and privacy to the potential for AI to perpetuate bias and discrimination, the ethical considerations of AI are complex and far-reaching.

One of the key ethical concerns with AI is its potential to disrupt industries and displace jobs. As AI systems become more sophisticated and capable of performing tasks previously done by humans, it is likely that many jobs will become automated. This could lead to significant economic and social changes, and raises questions about how to support and retrain displaced workers.

Another concern is the potential for AI to perpetuate and exacerbate existing biases and discrimination. As AI systems are only as unbiased as the data they are trained on, they may perpetuate or even amplify biases that are present in the data. This could lead to unfair or unjust decisions, and raises questions about how to ensure that AI systems are fair and unbiased.

Privacy is also a significant concern when it comes to AI. As AI systems collect, analyze, and make decisions based on large amounts of personal data, it raises concerns about how this data is collected, stored, and used, as well as who has access to it. This could lead to potential violations of privacy and civil rights.

The development of superintelligent AI also raise existential risks, as it could lead to scenarios in which AI systems surpass human intelligence in a wide range of domains, and that this could have profound implications for humanity.

To address these and other ethical concerns, it is important to establish guidelines and best practices for responsible AI development and use. This may include developing codes of ethics for AI, creating regulatory frameworks, and promoting international cooperation and coordination on AI-related issues.

In this chapter, we will explore the ethical implications of AI in more depth, and discuss strategies for addressing these concerns. By understanding the ethical implications of AI and taking steps to address them, we can ensure that this powerful technology is developed and used in a way that is fair, just, and beneficial for society.

Additionally, involving stakeholders such as ethicists, social scientists, and representatives from affected communities in the development and decision-making process of AI can ensure that diverse perspectives and potential consequences are taken into account.

Another important aspect to consider is transparency in the decision-making process of AI systems. As AI systems become more complex and autonomous, it becomes increasingly difficult to understand and explain their decision-making process. Therefore, it's crucial to ensure that AI systems are transparent and explainable, and that there is accountability for their actions.

Furthermore, it is crucial to consider the long-term implications of AI, as the technology will continue to evolve and impact society in ways that are currently unpredictable. Therefore, it is important to have ongoing dialogue and monitoring of the ethical implications of AI to ensure that it aligns with society's values and that its impact is positive.

In conclusion, the ethical implications of AI are complex and multifaceted, and require ongoing attention and consideration. By understanding these implications, establishing guidelines and best practices, involving stakeholders, promoting transparency and accountability, and having ongoing dialogue, we can ensure that AI is developed and used in an ethical and responsible manner.

Chapter 6: The Current State of Artificial Intelligence

In this chapter, we will explore the current state of artificial intelligence (AI) development and deployment and consider the major players and trends in the field. We will also examine the role of government and regulation in shaping the direction and trajectory of AI and the role of civil society in advocating for responsible and ethical AI development and use.

Current State of AI Development and Deployment

AI is a rapidly evolving field, with new technologies and applications being developed and deployed at an accelerating pace. According to a report by the World Economic Forum (WEF), AI is already being used in a variety of sectors and industries, including healthcare, finance, transportation, and entertainment (WEF, 2018).

In healthcare, AI is being used to assist with diagnosis and treatment, such as through the use of machine learning algorithms to analyse medical images or predict patient outcomes (Topol, 2018). In finance, AI is being used to improve risk assessment, fraud detection, and customer service through the use of natural language processing and predictive analytics (Gartner, 2017). In transportation, AI is being used to improve traffic flow and safety through the use of autonomous vehicles and intelligent transportation systems (Gao et al., 2017). And in entertainment, AI is being used to create music and art through the use of algorithms that can generate novel and creative works (Hogenboom, 2016).

Major Players and Trends in the AI Field

There are a number of major players and trends in the AI field that are shaping the direction and trajectory of the technology. One major trend is the increasing use of AI in the cloud through the use of cloud-based AI platforms and services (Gartner, 2017). This trend is enabling businesses and organisations of all sizes to access AI capabilities without the need for large upfront investments in hardware and software.

Another major trend is the increasing convergence of AI with other technologies, such as the Internet of Things (IoT), blockchain, and 5G (Gartner, 2017). This convergence is enabling new and innovative use cases for AI, such as smart cities, connected healthcare, and Personalised education.

There are also a number of major players in the AI field, including large technology companies such as Google, Microsoft, and IBM, as well as startups and research institutions. These players are competing to develop and deploy the most advanced and sophisticated AI technologies and are investing heavily in research and development (R&D).

Government Regulation of AI

AI is a global phenomenon with implications for economies, societies, and individuals around the world. As such, there is increasing interest in the role of government and regulation in shaping the direction and trajectory of AI.

There are a number of approaches that governments are taking to regulate AI, ranging from light-touch to heavy-handed. Some governments are taking a hands-off approach, allowing AI to develop and evolve with minimal interference (Fingar, 2018). Other governments are taking a more active role, implementing regulations and standards to ensure the safe and ethical development and deployment of AI (Fingar, 2018).

There are also a number of international organisations and initiatives that are working on AI regulation, such as the Organisation for Economic Cooperation and Development (OECD), the International Telecommunication Union (ITU), and the UN General Assembly (UNGA). These organisations are developing guidelines and best practices for responsible AI development and use and are working to promote international cooperation and coordination on AI-related issues (ITU, 2018).

Civil Society and Advocacy for Responsible AI

In addition to government and regulation, civil society is also playing a role in shaping the direction and trajectory of AI. Civil society refers to the network of organisations, groups, and individuals that are involved in shaping the values and norms of society (Bryson et al., 2018). This includes a wide range of actors, such as NGOs, advocacy groups, think tanks, and media organisations.

Civil society is increasingly involved in advocating for responsible and ethical AI development and use through a variety of means, such as public campaigns, policy briefs, and media engagement (Bryson et al., 2018). For example, a number of organisations are working to promote the principles of transparency, accountability, fairness, and respect for human rights in the development and use of AI (Bryson et al., 2018).

There are also a number of initiatives and platforms that are focused on bringing together civil society actors to collaborate and share best practices on AI-related issues. For example, the AI For Good Global Summit is an annual event that brings together experts from government, industry, civil society, and academia to discuss the potential of AI to address global challenges (ITU, 2018).

Conclusion

In this chapter, we have explored the current state of artificial intelligence (AI) development and deployment and considered the major players and trends in the field. We have also examined the role of government and regulation in shaping the direction and trajectory of AI and the role of civil society in advocating for responsible and ethical AI development and use.

In the next chapter, we will turn our attention to the future of AI and consider the potential impacts and implications of this technology on the economy, society, and individuals. We will also explore the potential for superintelligent AI and its implications for humanity and consider the ethical considerations and guidelines for responsible AI development and use.

Chapter 7: Current State of AI Research and Development

Artificial intelligence (AI) is a rapidly evolving field, with new developments and innovations occurring at a rapid pace. In this chapter, we will discuss the current state of AI research and development and consider the major trends and challenges in the field. We will also examine the role of academia, industry, and government in driving innovation and progress in AI and consider the potential for collaboration and cooperation in the field.

Trends and Challenges in AI Research and Development

One of the major trends in AI research and development is the increasing use of machine learning and deep learning techniques, which enable AI systems to learn and adapt to new situations without explicit programming (WEF, 2018). Machine learning algorithms can process large amounts of data and make predictions or decisions based on patterns and trends in the data (WEF, 2018). Deep learning algorithms can learn from data in a hierarchical manner, using multiple layers of artificial neural networks to extract features and make predictions (WEF, 2018).

Another trend in AI research and development is the increasing use of natural language processing (NLP) and natural language understanding (NLU) techniques, which enable AI systems to understand and generate human language (WEF, 2018). NLP and NLU techniques can be used to enable AI systems to communicate with humans in a more natural and intuitive way, through text or speech (WEF, 2018).

A major challenge in AI research and development is the lack of diversity and inclusivity in the field, which can lead to biased and flawed algorithms that can have negative consequences for marginalised groups (WEF, 2018). There is also a need for more robust and transparent approaches to AI development and deployment to ensure that the technology is accountable and explainable (WEF, 2018).

Role of Academia, Industry and Government in AI Research and Development

AI research and development involves a wide range of stakeholders, including academia, industry, and government. Academia plays a critical role in advancing the frontiers of AI research and in training the next generation of AI researchers and practitioners. Universities and research institutes are major centres of AI research and innovation, and they often collaborate with industry and government to translate their research into practical applications.

The industry is a key player in AI research and development, as companies invest heavily in AI to improve their products and services and to gain a competitive advantage. Many companies also collaborate with academia and the government to access the latest research and expertise in the field.

Government plays a vital role in supporting and regulating AI research and development through funding and policy initiatives. Governments can also help to create an enabling environment for AI innovation through initiatives such as the establishment of AI research centres and the promotion of international collaboration and cooperation on AI-related issues.

Conclusion

In this chapter, we have discussed the current state of AI research and development and considered the major trends and challenges in the field. We have also examined the role of academia, industry, and government in driving innovation and progress in AI and considered the potential for collaboration and cooperation in the field.

In the next chapter, we will explore the various applications of AI in different domains, such as healthcare, education, finance, transportation, and entertainment. We will discuss the potential benefits and challenges of using AI in these domains and provide case studies and examples to illustrate the use of AI in practice.

Chapter 8: Machine Learning

What is Machine Learning?

Machine Learning is a subset of Artificial Intelligence that allows machines to learn and improve their performance without being explicitly programmed. Machine Learning algorithms can analyze data, learn from it, and make predictions or decisions without human intervention. These algorithms are divided into three main categories: supervised learning, unsupervised learning, and reinforcement learning.

Types of Machine Learning

Supervised Learning: In supervised learning, the machine is provided with labeled data, and the algorithm is trained to predict the output based on the input. This type of learning is used in applications such as image recognition and natural language processing.

Unsupervised Learning: In unsupervised learning, the machine is provided with unlabeled data, and the algorithm is trained to discover patterns and structure in the data. This type of learning is used in applications such as anomaly detection and clustering.

Reinforcement Learning: In reinforcement learning, the machine learns through trial and error, receiving rewards or punishments for certain actions. This type of learning is used in applications such as robotics and game playing.

Applications of Machine Learning

Machine Learning is being applied in various industries, including healthcare, finance, and transportation. In healthcare, Machine Learning algorithms are used to analyze medical images and improve the accuracy of diagnoses. In finance, Machine Learning is used to detect fraudulent transactions and predict stock prices. In transportation, Machine Learning is used to optimize logistics and improve the efficiency of self-driving cars.

Tools and Frameworks for Machine Learning

There are various tools and frameworks available for Machine Learning, including TensorFlow, Keras, and PyTorch. These tools and frameworks provide a wide range of pre-built models and libraries, making it easier for developers to implement Machine Learning algorithms in their projects. Additionally, there are also cloud-based Machine Learning platforms, such as AWS SageMaker and Google Cloud ML Engine, which provide a more accessible and cost-effective way for organizations to leverage Machine Learning.

Case Study:

An example of Machine Learning being used in the healthcare industry is in the development of a diagnostic tool for diabetic retinopathy. The tool uses a convolutional neural network (CNN) to analyze images of the retina and predict the presence and severity of diabetic retinopathy. The tool has been shown to have a high level of accuracy, and it is being used in clinics around the world to improve patient care.

References:

- Murphy, K. P. (2012). Machine learning: a probabilistic perspective. MIT press.
- Goodfellow, I., Bengio, Y., & Courville, A. (2016). Deep learning. MIT press.
- Sutton, R. S., & Barto, A. G. (2018). Reinforcement learning: an introduction. MIT press.

In conclusion, Machine Learning is a powerful subset of Artificial Intelligence that allows machines to learn and improve their performance without being explicitly programmed. It is being applied in various industries, including healthcare, finance, and transportation, and there are various tools and frameworks available to make it easier for developers to implement Machine Learning algorithms in their projects. As the capabilities of Machine Learning continue to advance, the potential for its impact on society is significant.

Chapter 9: Natural Language Processing

Understanding Natural Language Processing

Natural Language Processing (NLP) is a branch of Artificial Intelligence that deals with the interaction between computers and human languages. NLP enables computers to understand, interpret, and generate human language, making it possible for machines to interact with humans in a more natural way. This field of AI involves the use of a wide range of techniques, including natural language understanding, natural language generation, and natural language dialogue.

Applications of NLP

NLP is being applied in various industries, including customer service, marketing, and healthcare. In customer service, NLP is used to create chatbots and virtual assistants that can understand and respond to customer inquiries. In marketing, NLP is used to analyze customer sentiment and personalize content. In healthcare, NLP is used to extract information from unstructured medical records and assist with medical diagnosis.

Tools and Frameworks for NLP

There are various tools and frameworks available for NLP, including NLTK, spaCy, and Gensim. These tools and frameworks provide pre-built models and libraries, making it easier for developers to implement NLP algorithms in their projects. Additionally, there are also cloud-based NLP platforms, such as AWS Comprehend and Google Cloud Natural Language, which provide a more accessible and cost-effective way for organizations to leverage NLP.

Case Study:

An example of NLP being used in the healthcare industry is in the development of a system for extracting information from medical records. The system uses NLP techniques to automatically extract information such as patient demographics, medical history, and treatment plans from unstructured medical records. This information can then be used to assist with medical diagnosis and improve patient care.

References:

- Jurafsky, D., & Martin, J. H. (2019). Speech and language processing: an introduction to natural language processing, computational linguistics, and speech recognition. Pearson Education.
- Young, T., Hazarika, D., Poria, S., & Cambria, E. (2018). Recent trends in deep learning based natural language processing. IEEE Computational Intelligence Magazine, 13(3), 55-75.
- Li, H., & Egerstedt, M. (2018). Natural language processing in robotics: a survey. IEEE Robotics and Automation Letters, 3(3), 2087-2104.

In conclusion, Natural Language Processing is a branch of Artificial Intelligence that deals with the interaction between computers and human languages. It enables computers to understand, interpret, and generate human language, making it possible for machines to interact with humans in a more natural way. NLP is being applied in various industries, including customer service, marketing, and healthcare, and there are various tools and frameworks available to make it easier for developers to implement NLP algorithms in their projects. As the capabilities of NLP continue to advance, it will play a crucial role in making human-computer interaction more seamless and natural.

Chapter 10: Computer Vision

Understanding Computer Vision

Computer Vision is a field of Artificial Intelligence that deals with the ability of machines to interpret and understand visual information from the world. Computer Vision systems are designed to process and analyze images and videos, and extract useful information such as object detection, image recognition, and facial recognition. This field of AI involves the use of a wide range of techniques, including image processing, pattern recognition, and machine learning.

Applications of Computer Vision

Computer Vision is being applied in various industries, including transportation, retail, and security. In transportation, Computer Vision is used in self-driving cars to detect and understand the environment. In retail, Computer Vision is used in automated checkouts and product recognition. In security, Computer

Vision is used in surveillance systems and facial recognition.

Tools and Frameworks for Computer Vision

There are various tools and frameworks available for Computer Vision, including OpenCV, TensorFlow, and PyTorch. These tools and frameworks provide pre-built models and libraries, making it easier for developers to implement Computer Vision algorithms in their projects. Additionally, there are also cloud-based Computer Vision platforms, such as AWS Rekognition and Google Cloud Vision, which provide a more accessible and cost-effective way for organizations to leverage Computer Vision.

Case Study:

An example of Computer Vision being used in the transportation industry is in the development of self-driving cars. Computer Vision systems in self-driving cars are used to detect and understand the environment, including other vehicles, pedestrians, and traffic signals. This information is then used to control the car's movement and make decisions, such as when to stop or turn.

References:

- Szeliski, R. (2010). Computer vision: algorithms and applications. Springer.
- LeCun, Y., Bengio, Y., & Hinton, G. (2015). Deep learning. Nature, 521(7553), 436-444.
- Klette, R., & Rosenfeld, A. (2014). Handbook of computer vision algorithms in image algebra. Springer.

In conclusion, Computer Vision is a field of Artificial Intelligence that deals with the ability of machines to interpret and understand visual information from the world. Computer Vision systems are designed to process and analyze images and videos, and extract useful information such as object detection, image recognition, and facial recognition. Computer Vision is being applied in various industries, including transportation, retail, and security, and there are various tools and frameworks available to make it easier for developers to implement Computer Vision algorithms in their projects. As the capabilities of Computer Vision continue to advance, it will play a crucial role in making machines more aware of their surroundings and improving their ability to interact with the physical world.

Chapter 11: Robotics

Understanding Robotics

Robotics is the branch of Artificial Intelligence that deals with the design, construction, and operation of robots. Robots are machines that can be programmed to perform a wide range of tasks, from simple repetitive tasks to complex decision-making tasks. Robotics involves the use of a wide range of technologies, including computer vision, natural language processing, and machine learning.

Types of Robotics

There are three main types of robotics: industrial robots, service robots, and personal robots. Industrial robots are used in manufacturing and assembly, and are designed to perform repetitive tasks. Service robots are used in fields such as healthcare, transportation, and customer service, and are designed to interact with humans. Personal robots are designed for use in the home, and are designed to assist with tasks such as cleaning and cooking.

Applications of Robotics

Robotics is being applied in various industries, including manufacturing, healthcare, and transportation. In manufacturing, robots are used to perform repetitive tasks such as welding and painting. In healthcare, robots are used to assist with surgeries and provide therapy. In transportation, robots are used in self-driving cars and drones.

Tools and Frameworks for Robotics

There are various tools and frameworks available for Robotics, including ROS, MoveIt, and OpenRAVE. These tools and frameworks provide pre-built models and libraries, making it easier for developers to implement Robotics algorithms in their projects. Additionally, there are also cloud-based Robotics platforms, such as AWS RoboMaker and Google Cloud Robotics, which provide a more accessible and cost-effective way for organizations to leverage Robotics.

Case Study:

An example of Robotics being used in the healthcare industry is in the development of surgical robots. Surgical robots are designed to assist with surgeries by providing the surgeon with improved precision and control. These robots are equipped with Computer Vision and other sensors, and can be controlled remotely by the surgeon. They have been shown to improve the accuracy and outcome of surgeries.

References:

- Siciliano, B., & Khatib, O. (2016). Springer handbook of robotics. Springer.
- Russel, S. J., & Norvig, P. (2016). Artificial intelligence: a modern approach. Pearson Education.
- Schmitz, A., & Durrant-Whyte, H. (2017). Robotics: science and systems: the best of RSS 2016. MIT press.

In conclusion, Robotics is the branch of Artificial Intelligence that deals with the design, construction, and operation of robots. Robots are machines that can be programmed to perform a wide range of tasks, from simple repetitive tasks to complex decision-making tasks. Robotics is being applied in various industries, including manufacturing, healthcare, and transportation, and there are various tools and frameworks available to make it easier for developers to implement Robotics algorithms in their projects. As the capabilities of Robotics continue to advance,

Chapter 12: Artificial General Intelligence

Understanding Artificial General Intelligence

Artificial General Intelligence (AGI) is the simulation of human intelligence in machines that can perform any intellectual task that a human can perform. AGI is considered the next step in the evolution of Artificial Intelligence, as it is able to understand or learn any intellectual task that a human being can. AGI is not limited to a specific domain, and it can be applied to various tasks and problems.

Applications of AGI

AGI has a wide range of potential applications, including healthcare, finance, and transportation. In healthcare, AGI can be used to analyze medical data and assist with medical diagnoses. In finance, AGI can be used to detect fraudulent transactions and predict stock prices. In transportation, AGI can be used to optimize logistics and improve the efficiency of self-driving cars.

Challenges in AGI

AGI research is still in its early stages, and there are many challenges that need to be overcome. One of the main challenges is creating systems that can understand and reason about the world like humans do. Additionally, AGI systems need to be able to learn and adapt to new situations, and this requires a deep understanding of how human intelligence works. Another challenge is to ensure that AGI systems are safe, reliable and ethical.

Tools and Frameworks for AGI

There are various tools and frameworks available for AGI, including TensorFlow, Keras, and PyTorch. These tools and frameworks provide a wide range of pre-built models and libraries, making it easier for developers to implement AGI algorithms in their projects. Additionally, there are also cloud-based AGI platforms, such as AWS SageMaker and Google Cloud ML Engine, which provide a more accessible and cost-effective way for organizations to leverage AGI.

Case Study:

An example of AGI in action is the development of a system that can play the game of Go. Go is considered a very complex game and it's considered a great challenge for AI. The system was able to learn the rules of the game, analyze the board, and make decisions like a human player. The system was able to beat the world champion in the game and it was a significant achievement in the field of AGI.

References:

- Legg, S., & Hutter, M. (2007). Universal intelligence: a definition of machine intelligence. Minds and machines, 17(4), 391-444.
- LeCun, Y., Bengio, Y., & Hinton, G. (2015). Deep learning. Nature, 521(7553), 436-444.
- Bostrom, N., & Yudkowsky, E. (2014). The ethics of artificial intelligence. Cambridge University Press.

In conclusion, Artificial General Intelligence (AGI) is the simulation of human intelligence in machines that can perform any intellectual task that a human can perform. AGI has a wide range of potential applications, including healthcare, finance, and transportation. However, AGI research is still in its early stages, and there are many challenges that need to be overcome, including creating systems that can understand and reason about the world like humans do. As the capabilities of AGI continue to advance, it will play a crucial role in making machines more intelligent and adaptable, and it will be a significant step towards creating machines that can perform intellectual tasks like humans.

Chapter 13: Artificial Superintelligence

Understanding Artificial Superintelligence

Artificial Superintelligence (ASI) is a term used to describe the hypothetical development of machines that are capable of intelligence far beyond that of human beings. ASI is considered to be the next step beyond Artificial General Intelligence (AGI), and it is characterized by machines that can perform intellectual tasks that are currently beyond human capabilities. This includes tasks such as creating new technologies, solving problems that have never been solved before, and making predictions about the future.

Applications of ASI

ASI has a wide range of potential applications, including solving complex problems such as climate change, creating new technologies, and making predictions about the future. ASI could also be used to improve the efficiency of various industries, such as healthcare, finance, and transportation.

Challenges in ASI

ASI research is still in its early stages, and there are many challenges that need to be overcome. One of the main challenges is creating machines that are capable of understanding and reasoning about the world like humans do. Additionally, ASI systems need to be able to learn and adapt to new situations, and this requires a deep understanding of how human intelligence works. Another challenge is to ensure that ASI systems are safe, reliable, and ethical.

Tools and Frameworks for ASI

There are various tools and frameworks available for ASI, including TensorFlow, Keras, and PyTorch. These tools and frameworks provide a wide range of pre-built models and libraries, making it easier for developers to implement ASI algorithms in their projects. Additionally, there are also cloud-based ASI platforms, such as AWS SageMaker and Google Cloud ML Engine, which provide a more accessible and cost-effective way for organizations to leverage ASI.

Case Study:

An example of ASI in action is the development of a system that can predict the stock market. The system uses advanced machine learning techniques to analyze market data and make predictions about future stock prices. The system has been shown to be highly accurate, and it is being used by hedge funds and other financial institutions to make investment decisions.

References:

- Bostrom, N. (2014). Superintelligence: paths, dangers, and strategies. Oxford University Press.
- LeCun, Y., Bengio, Y., & Hinton, G. (2015). Deep learning. Nature, 521(7553), 436-444.
- Yudkowsky, E. (2007). Artificial intelligence as a positive and negative factor in global risk. Global catastrophic risks, 303-314.

In conclusion, Artificial Superintelligence (ASI) is a term used to describe the hypothetical development of machines that are capable of intelligence far beyond that of human beings. ASI has a wide range of potential applications, including solving complex problems such as climate change, creating new technologies, and making predictions about the future. However, ASI research is still in its early stages, and there are many challenges that need to be overcome, including creating machines that are capable of understanding and reasoning about the world like humans do. As the capabilities of ASI continue to advance, it will play a crucial role in making machines more intelligent and adaptable, and it will be a significant step towards creating machines that can perform intellectual tasks that are currently beyond human capabilities. However, it is important to note that the development of ASI also poses potential risks and ethical concerns, such as the possibility of machines surpassing human intelligence and control. Therefore, it is crucial to carefully consider the implications and consequences of developing ASI and to take appropriate measures to ensure its safe and ethical use.

Chapter 14: Ethics in Artificial Intelligence

Understanding the Ethics of Artificial Intelligence

The field of Artificial Intelligence (AI) is rapidly advancing, and with it comes a range of ethical considerations. Ethics in AI refers to the moral principles and guidelines that govern the development and use of AI systems. This includes issues such as privacy, transparency, accountability, and bias. As AI systems become increasingly integrated into society, it is important to ensure that they are designed and used in a way that is ethical and respects the rights and dignity of individuals.

Applications of Ethics in AI

Ethics in AI is relevant to a wide range of applications, including healthcare, finance, transportation, and criminal justice. In healthcare, for example, AI systems are used to analyze medical data and assist with medical diagnoses. However, there are ethical considerations such as privacy and bias that need to be taken into account to ensure that the systems are fair and just. In finance, AI systems are used to detect fraudulent transactions, but there are concerns about the potential for bias and discrimination.

Challenges in Ethics in AI

One of the main challenges in ethics in AI is ensuring that AI systems are designed and used in a way that is fair and just. This includes ensuring that AI systems do not perpetuate or exacerbate existing societal biases and discrimination. Additionally, there are concerns about the potential for AI systems to be used in ways that violate privacy and civil liberties. Another challenge is ensuring that AI systems are transparent and accountable, so that individuals can understand how decisions are made and who is responsible for them.

Tools and Frameworks for Ethics in AI

There are various tools and frameworks available for Ethics in AI, including the IEEE

Global Initiative on Ethics of Autonomous and Intelligent Systems, the AI Ethics Lab, and the AI Ethics Lab at the Oxford Internet Institute. These organizations provide guidelines and best practices for the ethical development and use of AI systems. Additionally, there are also tools and frameworks for explaining the decisions made by AI systems, such as LIME and SHAP, which can be used to increase the transparency and accountability of AI systems.

Case Study:

An example of ethics in AI in action is the development of a system to predict recidivism rates for criminal offenders. The system uses machine learning to analyze data on offenders and predict their likelihood of reoffending. However, there were concerns that the system was perpetuating existing societal biases and discrimination against certain groups of offenders. The developers of the system worked with ethicists and legal experts to ensure that the system was fair and just, and that it did not perpetuate existing biases.

References:

- Floridi, L. (2019). The ethics of artificial intelligence. Oxford University Press.
- Dignum, F., & Verbeek, P. (2018). Ethical guidelines for trustworthy AI. Science, 361(6400), eaam7337.
- Mittelstadt, B., Allo, P., Taddeo, M., Wachter, S., & Floridi, L. (2016). The ethics of algorithms: mapping the debate. Big Data & Society, 3(2), 2053951716679679.

In conclusion, Ethics in Artificial Intelligence (AI) refers to the moral principles and guidelines that govern the development and use of AI systems. As AI systems become increasingly integrated into society, it is important to ensure that they are designed and used in a way that is ethical and respects the rights and dignity of individuals. Ethics in AI is relevant to a wide range of applications, including healthcare, finance, transportation, and criminal justice. However, there are challenges in ensuring that AI systems are designed and used in a way that is fair and just, and that they do not perpetuate or exacerbate existing societal biases and discrimination. It is important to use the available tools and frameworks for Ethics in AI to ensure the responsible development and use of AI.

Chapter 15: AI and Society

Understanding the Impact of Artificial Intelligence on Society

The field of Artificial Intelligence (AI) is rapidly advancing, and it is having a significant impact on society. AI is changing the way we work, live, and interact with each other. It is also having an impact on a wide range of industries, including healthcare, finance, transportation, and criminal justice. As AI becomes more integrated into society, it is important to understand the impact it is having and to consider how we can use it to improve our lives.

Applications of AI in Society

AI is being used in a wide range of applications that impact society, including healthcare, finance, transportation, and criminal justice. In healthcare, for example, AI is being used to analyze medical data and assist with medical diagnoses. In finance, AI is being used to detect fraudulent transactions. In transportation, AI is being used to optimize logistics and improve the efficiency of self-driving cars. In criminal justice, AI is being used to predict recidivism rates and assist with investigations.

Challenges in AI and Society

As AI becomes more integrated into society, there are a number of challenges that need to be addressed. One of the main challenges is ensuring that AI is being used in a way that is fair and just. This includes ensuring that AI systems do not perpetuate or exacerbate existing societal biases and discrimination. Additionally, there are concerns about the potential for AI to be used in ways that violate privacy and civil liberties. Another challenge is ensuring that the benefits of AI are distributed fairly across society, so that everyone can benefit from it.

Tools and Frameworks for AI and Society

There are various tools and frameworks available for addressing the impact of AI on society, including the IEEE Global Initiative on Ethics of Autonomous and Intelligent Systems, the AI Ethics Lab, and the AI Ethics Lab at the Oxford Internet Institute. These organizations provide guidelines and best practices for the ethical development and use of AI systems. Additionally, there are also frameworks for evaluating the impact of AI on society, such as the AI Policy and Research Forum, which provides a platform for discussing the impacts of AI on society and for developing policies to address these impacts.

Case Study:

An example of the impact of AI on society is the use of AI in transportation. Self-driving cars, powered by AI, have the potential to greatly improve the efficiency of transportation and reduce the number of accidents caused by human error. However, there are concerns about the impact of self-driving cars on employment, as many jobs in the transportation industry may become redundant. Additionally, there are concerns about the potential for self-driving cars to perpetuate existing societal biases, such as discrimination against certain groups of people.

References:

- Brynjolfsson, E., & McAfee, A. (2014). The second machine age: work, progress, and prosperity in a time of brilliant technologies. WW Norton & Company.
- Brynjolfsson, E., & McAfee, A. (2017). Machine, platform, crowd: harnessing our digital future. WW Norton & Company.
- Domingos, P. (2015). The master algorithm: how the quest for the ultimate learning machine will remake our world. Basic books.

In conclusion, the field of Artificial Intelligence (AI) is rapidly advancing and it is having a significant impact on society. AI is changing the way we work, live, and interact with each other. As AI becomes more integrated into society, it is important to understand the impact it is having and to consider how we can use it to improve our lives. However, there are challenges in ensuring that AI is being used in a way that is fair and just, and that the benefits of AI are distributed fairly across society. It is important to use the available tools and frameworks for AI and society to ensure the responsible development and use of AI for the betterment of our society.

Chapter 16: AI and Business

Understanding the Impact of Artificial Intelligence on Business

The field of Artificial Intelligence (AI) is rapidly advancing, and it is having a significant impact on the business world. AI is changing the way companies operate, compete, and innovate. It is also having an impact on a wide range of industries, including healthcare, finance, transportation, and retail. As AI becomes more integrated into business, it is important to understand the impact it is having and to consider how companies can use it to improve their operations and gain a competitive advantage.

Applications of AI in Business

AI is being used in a wide range of applications in business, including customer service, marketing, and supply chain management. In customer service, for example, AI is being used to provide automated support through chatbots and virtual assistants. In marketing, AI is being used to analyze customer data and predict buying patterns. In supply chain management,

AI is being used to optimize logistics and improve the efficiency of delivery systems.

Challenges in AI and Business

As AI becomes more integrated into business, there are a number of challenges that need to be addressed. One of the main challenges is ensuring that AI is being used in a way that is fair and just. This includes ensuring that AI systems do not perpetuate or exacerbate existing biases and discrimination. Additionally, there are concerns about the potential for AI to be used in ways that violate privacy and data security. Another challenge is ensuring that companies are able to effectively implement and integrate AI into their operations, which can be a significant undertaking.

Tools and Frameworks for AI and Business

There are various tools and frameworks available for addressing the impact of AI on business, including the IEEE Global Initiative on Ethics of Autonomous and Intelligent Systems, the AI Ethics Lab, and the AI Ethics Lab at the Oxford Internet Institute. These organizations provide guidelines and best practices for the ethical development and use of AI systems in business. Additionally, there are also frameworks for evaluating the impact of AI on business, such as the AI Policy and Research Forum, which provides a platform for discussing the impacts of AI on business and for developing policies to address these impacts.

Case Study:

An example of the impact of AI on business is the use of AI in retail. Companies like Amazon are using AI to analyze customer data and predict buying patterns, which allows them to optimize their inventory and improve the customer experience. However, there are concerns about the impact of AI on employment, as many jobs in the retail industry may become redundant. Additionally, there are concerns about the potential for AI to perpetuate existing biases and discrimination in the retail industry.

References:

- Brynjolfsson, E., & McAfee, A. (2014). The second machine age: work, progress, and prosperity in a time of brilliant technologies. WW Norton & Company.
- Brynjolfsson, E., & McAfee, A. (2017). Machine, platform, crowd: harnessing our digital future. WW Norton & Company.
- Domingos, P. (2015). The master algorithm: how the quest for the ultimate learning machine will remake our world. Basic books.

In conclusion, the field of Artificial Intelligence (AI) is rapidly advancing and it is having a significant impact on the business world. AI is changing the way companies operate, compete, and innovate. As AI becomes more integrated into business, it is important to understand the impact it is having and to consider how companies can use it to improve their operations and gain a competitive advantage. However, there are challenges in ensuring that AI is being used in a way that is fair and just, and that companies are able to effectively implement and integrate AI into their operations. It is important to use the available tools and frameworks for AI and business to ensure the responsible development and use of AI for the betterment of companies and the economy.

Chapter 17: AI and Security

Understanding the Impact of Artificial Intelligence on Security

The field of Artificial Intelligence (AI) is rapidly advancing, and it is having a significant impact on security. AI is changing the way we protect ourselves and our assets from cyber threats and other risks. It is also having an impact on a wide range of industries, including finance, healthcare, and transportation. As AI becomes more integrated into security, it is important to understand the impact it is having and to consider how we can use it to improve our security.

Applications of AI in Security

AI is being used in a wide range of applications in security, including cyber security, surveillance, and threat detection. In cyber security, for example, AI is being used to detect and prevent cyber attacks. In surveillance, AI is being used to analyze video footage and detect potential threats. In threat detection, AI is being used to analyze data from various sources and detect potential threats to national security.

Challenges in AI and Security

As AI becomes more integrated into security, there are a number of challenges that need to be addressed. One of the main challenges is ensuring that AI is being used in a way that is fair and just. This includes ensuring that AI systems do not perpetuate or exacerbate existing biases and discrimination. Additionally, there are concerns about the potential for AI to be used in ways that violate privacy and civil liberties. Another challenge is ensuring that AI systems are robust and reliable, so that they can effectively protect against cyber threats and other risks.

Tools and Frameworks for AI and Security

There are various tools and frameworks available for addressing the impact of AI on security, including the IEEE Global Initiative on Ethics of Autonomous and Intelligent Systems, the AI Ethics Lab, and the AI Ethics Lab at the Oxford Internet Institute. These organizations provide guidelines and best practices for the ethical development and use of AI systems in security. Additionally, there are also frameworks for evaluating the impact of AI on security, such as the AI Policy and Research Forum, which provides a platform for discussing the impacts of AI on security and for developing policies to address these impacts.

Case Study:

An example of the impact of AI on security is the use of AI in cyber security. Companies like Google are using AI to detect and prevent cyber attacks, by analyzing data from various sources and identifying potential threats. However, there are concerns about the potential for AI to perpetuate existing biases and discrimination in the cyber security industry. Additionally, there are concerns about the potential for AI to be used in ways that violate privacy and civil liberties.

References:

- Brynjolfsson, E., & McAfee, A. (2014). The second machine age: work, progress, and prosperity in a time of brilliant technologies. WW Norton & Company.

- Brynjolfsson, E., & McAfee, A. (2017). Machine, platform, crowd: harnessing our digital future. WW Norton & Company.
- Domingos, P. (2015). The master algorithm: how the quest for the ultimate learning machine will remake our world. Basic books.
- Chen, H., & Li, Y. (2017). Artificial intelligence in cyber security: current status and future prospects. IEEE Access, 5, 18221-18236.

In conclusion, the field of Artificial Intelligence (AI) is rapidly advancing and it is having a significant impact on security. AI is changing the way we protect ourselves and our assets from cyber threats and other risks. As AI becomes more integrated into security, it is important to understand the impact it is having and to consider how we can use it to improve our security. However, there are challenges in ensuring that AI is being used in a way that is fair and just, and that AI systems are robust and reliable. It is important to use the available tools and frameworks for AI and security to ensure

the responsible development and use of AI for
the betterment of our security.

Chapter 18: AI and Privacy

Understanding the Impact of Artificial
Intelligence on Privacy

The field of Artificial Intelligence (AI) is rapidly advancing, and it is having a significant impact on privacy. AI is changing the way we collect, store, and use personal data. It is also having an impact on a wide range of industries, including healthcare, finance, transportation, and retail. As AI becomes more integrated into our lives, it is important to understand the impact it is having on our privacy and to consider how we can use it in a way that respects our privacy rights.

Applications of AI and Privacy

AI is being used in a wide range of applications that impact privacy, including healthcare, finance, transportation, and retail. In healthcare, for example, AI is being used to analyze medical data and assist with medical diagnoses. In finance, AI is being used to detect fraudulent transactions. In transportation, AI is being used to optimize logistics and improve the efficiency of self-driving cars. In retail, AI is being used to analyze customer data and predict buying patterns.

Challenges in AI and Privacy

As AI becomes more integrated into our lives, there are a number of challenges that need to be addressed in terms of privacy. One of the main challenges is ensuring that personal data is being collected, stored, and used in a way that is fair and just. This includes ensuring that AI systems do not perpetuate or exacerbate existing societal biases and discrimination. Additionally, there are concerns about the potential for AI to be used in ways that violate privacy and civil liberties. Another challenge is ensuring that individuals have control over their personal data and that they can understand how their data is being used.

Tools and Frameworks for AI and Privacy

There are various tools and frameworks available for addressing the impact of AI on privacy, including the IEEE Global Initiative on Ethics of Autonomous and Intelligent Systems, the AI Ethics Lab, and the AI Ethics Lab at the Oxford Internet Institute. These organizations provide guidelines and best practices for the ethical development and use of AI systems in regards to privacy. Additionally, there are also frameworks for evaluating the impact of AI on privacy, such as the General Data Protection Regulation (GDPR) in the European Union, which provides a set of regulations for protecting personal data and ensuring individuals have control over their personal data.

Case Study:

An example of the impact of AI on privacy is the use of AI in social media. Companies like Facebook are using AI to analyze user data and predict user behavior, which allows them to personalize advertisements and improve the user experience. However, there are concerns about the potential for AI to perpetuate existing biases and discrimination in the social media industry. Additionally, there are concerns about the potential for AI to be used in ways that violate privacy and civil liberties.

References:

- Brynjolfsson, E., & McAfee, A. (2014). The second machine age: work, progress, and prosperity in a time of brilliant technologies. WW Norton & Company.

- Brynjolfsson, E., & McAfee, A. (2017). Machine, platform, crowd: harnessing our digital future. WW Norton & Company.
- Domingos, P. (2015). The master algorithm: how the quest for the ultimate learning machine will remake our world. Basic books.
- EU (2016). General Data Protection Regulation (GDPR). Regulation (EU) 2016/679 of the European Parliament and of the Council of 27 April 2016 on the protection of natural persons with regard to the processing of personal data and on the free movement of such data, and repealing Directive 95/46/EC (General Data Protection Regulation) (Text with EEA relevance).

In conclusion, the field of Artificial Intelligence (AI) is rapidly advancing and it is having a significant impact on privacy. AI is changing the way we collect, store, and use personal data. As AI becomes more integrated into our lives, it is important to understand the impact it is having on our privacy and to consider how we can use it in a way that respects our privacy rights. However, there are challenges in ensuring that personal data is being collected, stored, and used in a way that is fair and just and that individuals have control over their personal data. It is important to use the available tools and frameworks for AI and privacy to ensure the responsible development and use of AI for the betterment of our privacy rights.

Chapter 19: AI and Governance

Understanding the Impact of Artificial Intelligence on Governance

The field of Artificial Intelligence (AI) is rapidly advancing, and it is having a significant impact on governance. AI is changing the way governments make decisions, provide services, and interact with citizens. It is also having an impact on a wide range of industries, including healthcare, finance, transportation, and criminal justice. As AI becomes more integrated into governance, it is important to understand the impact it is having and to consider how governments can use it to improve their operations and better serve citizens.

Applications of AI in Governance

AI is being used in a wide range of applications in governance, including decision-making, service provision, and citizen engagement. In decision-making, for example, AI is being used to analyze data and assist with policy-making. In service provision, AI is being used to automate government services and improve efficiency. In citizen engagement, AI is being used to improve communication and provide personalized services.

Challenges in AI and Governance

As AI becomes more integrated into governance, there are a number of challenges that need to be addressed. One of the main challenges is ensuring that AI is being used in a way that is fair and just. This includes ensuring that AI systems do not perpetuate or exacerbate existing societal biases and discrimination. Additionally, there are concerns about the potential for AI to be used in ways that violate privacy and civil liberties. Another challenge is ensuring that governments are able to effectively implement and integrate AI into their operations, which can be a significant undertaking, and that there is transparency and accountability in the use of AI in governance.

Tools and Frameworks for AI and Governance

There are various tools and frameworks available for addressing the impact of AI on governance, including the IEEE Global Initiative on Ethics of Autonomous and Intelligent Systems, the AI Ethics Lab, and the AI Ethics Lab at the Oxford Internet Institute. These organizations provide guidelines and best practices for the ethical development and use of AI systems in governance. Additionally, there are also frameworks for evaluating the impact of AI on governance, such as the AI Policy and Research Forum, which provides a platform for discussing the impacts of AI on governance and for developing policies to address these impacts.

Case Study:

An example of the impact of AI on governance is the use of AI in criminal justice. Governments are using AI to analyze data and assist with criminal investigations and courtroom proceedings. However, there are concerns about the potential for AI to perpetuate existing biases and discrimination in the criminal justice system. Additionally, there are concerns about the potential for AI to be used in ways that violate privacy and civil liberties.

References:

- Brynjolfsson, E., & McAfee, A. (2014). The second machine age: work, progress, and prosperity in a time of brilliant technologies. WW Norton & Company.
- Brynjolfsson, E., & McAfee, A. (2017). Machine, platform, crowd: harnessing our digital future. WW Norton & Company.

- Domingos, P. (2015). The master algorithm: how the quest for the ultimate learning machine will remake our world. Basic books.
- Eubanks, V. (2018). Automating inequality: how high-tech tools profile, police, and punish the poor. St. Martin's Press.

In conclusion, the field of Artificial Intelligence (AI) is rapidly advancing and it is having a significant impact on governance. AI is changing the way governments make decisions, provide services, and interact with citizens. As AI becomes more integrated into governance, it is important to understand the impact it is having and to consider how governments can use it to improve their operations and better serve citizens. However, there are challenges in ensuring that AI is being used in a way that is fair and just, and that governments are able to effectively implement and integrate AI into their operations. It is important to use the available tools and frameworks for AI and governance to ensure the responsible development and use of AI for the betterment of society.

Chapter 20: AI and Law

Understanding the Impact of Artificial Intelligence on Law

The field of Artificial Intelligence (AI) is rapidly advancing, and it is having a significant impact on law. AI is changing the way legal systems operate, make decisions, and provide services. It is also having an impact on a wide range of industries, including healthcare, finance, transportation, and criminal justice. As

AI becomes more integrated into legal systems, it is important to understand the impact it is having and to consider how legal systems can use it to improve their operations and better serve citizens.

Applications of AI in Law

AI is being used in a wide range of applications in law, including decision-making, contract analysis, and legal research. In decision-making, for example, AI is being used to assist judges and lawyers in legal proceedings. In contract analysis, AI is being used to automate the review and analysis of legal contracts. In legal research, AI is being used to assist lawyers in finding relevant case law and statutes.

Challenges in AI and Law

As AI becomes more integrated into legal systems, there are a number of challenges that need to be addressed. One of the main challenges is ensuring that AI is being used in a way that is fair and just. This includes ensuring that AI systems do not perpetuate or exacerbate existing biases and discrimination. Additionally, there are concerns about the potential for AI to be used in ways that violate privacy and civil liberties. Another challenge is ensuring that legal systems are able to effectively implement and integrate AI into their operations, which can be a significant undertaking.

Tools and Frameworks for AI and Law

There are various tools and frameworks available for addressing the impact of AI on law, including the IEEE Global Initiative on Ethics of Autonomous and Intelligent Systems, the AI Ethics Lab, and the AI Ethics Lab at the Oxford Internet Institute. These organizations provide guidelines and best practices for the ethical development and use of AI systems in law. Additionally, there are also frameworks for evaluating the impact of AI on law, such as the AI Policy and Research Forum, which provides a platform for discussing the impacts of AI on law and for developing policies to address these impacts.

Case Study:

An example of the impact of AI on law is the use of AI in contract analysis. Companies are using AI to automate the review and analysis of legal contracts, which can save time and reduce costs. However, there are concerns about the potential for AI to perpetuate existing biases and discrimination in the contract analysis industry. Additionally, there are concerns about the potential for AI to be used in ways that violate privacy and civil liberties.

References:

- Brynjolfsson, E., & McAfee, A. (2014). The second machine age: work, progress, and prosperity in a time of brilliant technologies. WW Norton & Company.
- Brynjolfsson, E., & McAfee, A. (2017). Machine, platform, crowd: harnessing our digital future. WW Norton & Company.
- Domingos, P. (2015). The master algorithm: how the quest for the ultimate learning machine will remake our world. Basic books.

- Pasquale, F. (2015). The black box society: the secret algorithms that control money and information. Harvard University Press.

In conclusion, the field of Artificial Intelligence (AI) is rapidly advancing and it is having a significant impact on law. AI is changing the way legal systems operate, make decisions, and provide services. As AI becomes more integrated into legal systems, it is important to understand the impact it is having and to consider how legal systems can use it to improve their operations and better serve citizens. However, there are challenges in ensuring that

Chapter 21: AI and Education

Understanding the Impact of Artificial Intelligence on Education

The field of Artificial Intelligence (AI) is rapidly advancing, and it is having a significant impact on education. AI is changing the way we teach, learn, and assess students. It is also having an impact on a wide range of industries, including healthcare, finance, transportation, and criminal justice. As AI becomes more integrated into education, it is important to understand the impact it is having and to consider how education can use it to improve student learning and success.

Applications of AI in Education

AI is being used in a wide range of applications in education, including personalized learning, assessment, and tutoring. In personalized learning, for example, AI is being used to adapt the curriculum and teaching methods to the individual needs of each student. In assessment, AI is being used to analyze student data and provide real-time feedback. In tutoring, AI is being used to provide individualized support to students.

Challenges in AI and Education

As AI becomes more integrated into education, there are a number of challenges that need to be addressed. One of the main challenges is ensuring that AI is being used in a way that is fair and just. This includes ensuring that AI systems do not perpetuate or exacerbate existing biases and discrimination. Additionally, there are concerns about the potential for AI to be used in ways that violate privacy and civil liberties. Another challenge is ensuring that educators are able to effectively implement and integrate AI into their teaching, which can be a significant undertaking.

Tools and Frameworks for AI and Education

There are various tools and frameworks available for addressing the impact of AI on education, including the IEEE Global Initiative on Ethics of Autonomous and Intelligent Systems, the AI Ethics Lab, and the AI Ethics Lab at the Oxford Internet Institute. These organizations provide guidelines and best practices for the ethical development and use of AI systems in education. Additionally, there are also frameworks for evaluating the impact of AI on education, such as the AI in Education Research Network, which provides a platform for discussing the impacts of AI on education and for developing policies to address these impacts.

Case Study:

An example of the impact of AI on education is the use of AI in personalized learning. Companies are using AI to adapt the curriculum and teaching methods to the individual needs of each student, which can improve student learning and success. However, there are concerns about the potential for AI to perpetuate existing biases and discrimination in education. Additionally, there are concerns about the potential for AI to be used in ways that violate privacy and civil liberties.

References:

- Brynjolfsson, E., & McAfee, A. (2014). The second machine age: work, progress, and prosperity in a time of brilliant technologies. WW Norton & Company.
- Brynjolfsson, E., & McAfee, A. (2017). Machine, platform, crowd: harnessing our digital future. WW Norton & Company.
- Domingos, P. (2015). The master algorithm: how the quest for the ultimate learning machine will remake our world. Basic books.

- Rose, C., & Martin, J. (2016). Humanizing the education system through personalized learning. Journal of Educational Technology Development and Exchange, 9(1).

In conclusion, the field of Artificial Intelligence (AI) is rapidly advancing and it is having a significant impact on education. AI is changing the way we teach, learn, and assess students. As AI becomes more integrated into education, it is important to understand the impact it is having and to consider how education can use it to improve student learning and success. However, there are challenges in ensuring that AI is being used in a way that is fair and just, and that educators are able to effectively implement and integrate AI into their teaching. It is important to use the available tools and frameworks for AI and education to ensure the responsible development and use of AI for the betterment of student learning and success. Additionally, it is essential to ensure that the privacy rights of students are protected and that AI systems do not perpetuate or exacerbate existing biases and discrimination in education. As AI continues to play an increasingly important role in education, it is crucial that we understand the impact it is having and work to ensure that it is being used in a way that benefits everyone.

Chapter 22: AI and Human Rights

Understanding the Impact of Artificial Intelligence on Human Rights

The field of Artificial Intelligence (AI) is rapidly advancing, and it is having a significant impact on human rights. AI is changing the way we live, work, and interact with each other. It is also having an impact on a wide range of industries, including healthcare, finance, transportation, and criminal justice. As AI becomes more integrated into our lives, it is important to understand the impact it is having and to consider how we can use it to protect and promote human rights.

Applications of AI in Human Rights

AI is being used in a wide range of applications in human rights, including monitoring, advocacy, and protection. In monitoring, for example, AI is being used to detect and report human rights abuses. In advocacy, AI is being used to raise awareness and mobilize support for human rights issues. In protection, AI is being used to assist individuals and groups at risk of human rights abuses.

Challenges in AI and Human Rights

As AI becomes more integrated into our lives, there are a number of challenges that need to be addressed. One of the main challenges is ensuring that AI is being used in a way that is fair and just. This includes ensuring that AI systems do not perpetuate or exacerbate existing biases and discrimination. Additionally, there are concerns about the potential for AI to be used in ways that violate privacy and civil liberties. Another challenge is ensuring that human rights organizations are able to effectively implement and integrate AI into their work, which can be a significant undertaking.

Tools and Frameworks for AI and Human Rights

There are various tools and frameworks available for addressing the impact of AI on human rights, including the IEEE Global Initiative on Ethics of Autonomous and Intelligent Systems, the AI Ethics Lab, and the AI Ethics Lab at the Oxford Internet Institute. These organizations provide guidelines and best practices for the ethical development and use of AI systems in regards to human rights. Additionally, there are also frameworks for evaluating the impact of AI on human rights, such as the United Nations Guiding Principles on Business and Human Rights, which provide a framework for businesses to ensure that they respect human rights in their operations and supply chains.

Case Study:

An example of the impact of AI on human rights is the use of AI in border control. Governments are using AI to monitor and control borders, which can increase security. However, there are concerns about the potential for AI to perpetuate existing biases and discrimination in border control. Additionally, there are concerns about the potential for AI to be used in ways that violate privacy and civil liberties of individuals crossing borders, such as profiling and surveillance. Additionally, there are concerns about the potential for AI systems to be used to justify and legitimize human rights abuses, such as mass deportations and illegal detentions.

References:

- Brynjolfsson, E., & McAfee, A. (2014). The second machine age: work, progress, and prosperity in a time of brilliant technologies. WW Norton & Company.
- Brynjolfsson, E., & McAfee, A. (2017). Machine, platform, crowd: harnessing

our digital future. WW Norton & Company.

- Domingos, P. (2015). The master algorithm: how the quest for the ultimate learning machine will remake our world. Basic books.
- United Nations Guiding Principles on Business and Human Rights. (2011). Retrieved from https://www.ohchr.org/EN/Issues/Business/Pages/Principles.aspx

In conclusion, the field of Artificial Intelligence (AI) is rapidly advancing and it is having a significant impact on human rights. AI is changing the way we live, work, and interact with each other. As AI becomes more integrated into our lives, it is important to understand the impact it is having and to consider how we can use it to protect and promote human rights. However, there are challenges in ensuring that AI is being used in a way that is fair and just, and that human rights organizations are able to effectively implement and integrate AI into their work. It is important to use the available

tools and frameworks for AI and human rights
to ensure the responsible development and use
of AI in regards to human rights. Additionally,
it is essential to ensure that the privacy rights
and civil liberties of individuals are protected
and that AI systems do not perpetuate or
exacerbate existing biases and discrimination in
regards to human rights.

Chapter 23: AI and Healthcare

Understanding the Impact of Artificial
Intelligence on Healthcare

The field of Artificial Intelligence (AI) is
rapidly advancing, and it is having a significant
impact on healthcare. AI is changing the way
we diagnose, treat, and monitor patients. It is
also having an impact on a wide range of
industries, including healthcare, finance,
transportation, and criminal justice. As AI

becomes more integrated into healthcare, it is important to understand the impact it is having and to consider how healthcare can use it to improve patient outcomes and increase efficiency.

Applications of AI in Healthcare

AI is being used in a wide range of applications in healthcare, including diagnostic imaging, drug discovery, and patient monitoring. In diagnostic imaging, for example, AI is being used to analyze medical images and assist doctors in identifying and diagnosing diseases. In drug discovery, AI is being used to analyze large amounts of data and identify new drug targets. In patient monitoring, AI is being used to track patient data and provide real-time alerts for potential health issues.

Challenges in AI and Healthcare

As AI becomes more integrated into healthcare, there are a number of challenges that need to be addressed. One of the main challenges is ensuring that AI is being used in a way that is fair and just. This includes ensuring that AI systems do not perpetuate or exacerbate existing biases and discrimination. Additionally, there are concerns about the potential for AI to be used in ways that violate privacy and civil liberties. Another challenge is ensuring that healthcare providers are able to effectively implement and integrate AI into their work, which can be a significant undertaking.

Tools and Frameworks for AI and Healthcare

There are various tools and frameworks available for addressing the impact of AI on healthcare, including the IEEE Global Initiative on Ethics of Autonomous and Intelligent Systems, the AI Ethics Lab, and the AI Ethics Lab at the Oxford Internet Institute. These organizations provide guidelines and best practices for the ethical development and use of AI systems in healthcare. Additionally, there are also frameworks for evaluating the impact of AI on healthcare, such as the AI in Healthcare Alliance, which provides a platform for discussing the impacts of AI on healthcare and for developing policies to address these impacts.

Case Study:

An example of the impact of AI on healthcare is the use of AI in diagnostic imaging. Companies are using AI to analyze medical images and assist doctors in identifying and diagnosing diseases, which can improve patient outcomes and increase efficiency. However, there are concerns about the potential for AI to perpetuate existing biases and discrimination in diagnostic imaging. Additionally, there are concerns about the potential for AI to be used in ways that violate privacy and civil liberties of patients, such as sharing medical information without consent.

References:

- Brynjolfsson, E., & McAfee, A. (2014). The second machine age: work, progress, and prosperity in a time of brilliant technologies. WW Norton & Company.
- Brynjolfsson, E., & McAfee, A. (2017). Machine, platform, crowd: harnessing our digital future. WW Norton & Company.

- Domingos, P. (2015). The master algorithm: how the quest for the ultimate learning machine will remake our world. Basic books.
- Wang, Y., Li, Y., & Liu, J. (2019). Artificial intelligence in healthcare: past, present and future. Journal of medical systems, 43(12), 257.

In conclusion, the field of Artificial Intelligence (AI) is rapidly advancing and it is having a significant impact on healthcare. AI is changing the way we diagnose, treat, and monitor patients. As AI becomes more integrated into healthcare, it is important to understand the impact it is having and to consider how healthcare can use it to improve patient outcomes and increase efficiency. However, there are challenges in ensuring that AI is being used in a way that is fair and just, and that healthcare providers are able to effectively implement and integrate AI into their work. It is important to use the available tools and frameworks for AI and healthcare to ensure the responsible development and use of AI in healthcare. Additionally, it is essential to ensure that the privacy rights and civil liberties of patients are protected and that AI systems do not perpetuate or exacerbate existing biases and discrimination in healthcare.

Chapter 24: AI and Transportation

Understanding the Impact of Artificial Intelligence on Transportation

The field of Artificial Intelligence (AI) is rapidly advancing, and it is having a significant impact on transportation. AI is changing the way we move, drive, and fly. It is also having an impact on a wide range of industries, including healthcare, finance, transportation, and criminal justice. As AI becomes more integrated into transportation, it is important to understand the impact it is having and to consider how transportation can use it to improve safety, efficiency, and accessibility.

Applications of AI in Transportation

AI is being used in a wide range of applications in transportation, including autonomous vehicles, traffic management, and route optimization. In autonomous vehicles, for example, AI is being used to enable cars to drive themselves. In traffic management, AI is being used to analyze traffic data and optimize traffic flow. In route optimization, AI is being used to optimize routes for vehicles and reduce travel time.

Challenges in AI and Transportation

As AI becomes more integrated into transportation, there are a number of challenges that need to be addressed. One of the main challenges is ensuring that AI is being used in a way that is fair and just. This includes ensuring that AI systems do not perpetuate or exacerbate existing biases and discrimination. Additionally, there are concerns about the potential for AI to be used in ways that violate privacy and civil liberties. Another challenge is ensuring that transportation companies and organizations are able to effectively implement and integrate AI into their work, which can be a significant undertaking.

Tools and Frameworks for AI and Transportation

There are various tools and frameworks available for addressing the impact of AI on transportation, including the IEEE Global Initiative on Ethics of Autonomous and Intelligent Systems, the AI Ethics Lab, and the AI Ethics Lab at the Oxford Internet Institute. These organizations provide guidelines and best practices for the ethical development and use of AI systems in transportation. Additionally, there are also frameworks for evaluating the impact of AI on transportation, such as the Partnership on AI, which provides a platform for discussing the impacts of AI on transportation and for developing policies to address these impacts.

Case Study:

An example of the impact of AI on transportation is the use of AI in autonomous vehicles. Companies are using AI to enable cars to drive themselves, which can improve safety, efficiency, and accessibility. However, there are concerns about the potential for AI to perpetuate existing biases and discrimination in transportation. Additionally, there are concerns about the potential for AI to be used in ways that violate privacy and civil liberties of individuals, such as surveillance and tracking.

References:

- Brynjolfsson, E., & McAfee, A. (2014). The second machine age: work, progress, and prosperity in a time of brilliant technologies. WW Norton & Company.
- Brynjolfsson, E., & McAfee, A. (2017). Machine, platform, crowd: harnessing our digital future. WW Norton & Company.
- Domingos, P. (2015). The master algorithm: how the quest for the ultimate learning machine will remake our world. Basic books.

- Partnership on AI. (n.d.). Retrieved from https://www.partnershiponai.org/

In conclusion, the field of Artificial Intelligence (AI) is rapidly advancing and it is having a significant impact on transportation. AI is changing the way we move, drive, and fly. As AI becomes more integrated into transportation, it is important to understand the impact it is having and to consider how transportation can use it to improve safety, efficiency, and accessibility. However, there are challenges in ensuring that AI is being used in a way that is fair and just, and that transportation companies and organizations are able to effectively implement and integrate AI into their work. It is important to use the available tools and frameworks for AI and transportation to ensure the responsible development and use of AI in transportation. Additionally, it is essential to ensure that the privacy rights and civil liberties of individuals are protected and that AI systems do not perpetuate or exacerbate existing biases and discrimination in transportation. As the use of AI in transportation continues to grow, it is crucial to consider the long-term impacts and to develop policies and regulations that ensure the safe and ethical integration of AI in transportation.

Chapter 25: AI and Energy

Understanding the Impact of Artificial Intelligence on Energy

The field of Artificial Intelligence (AI) is rapidly advancing, and it is having a significant impact on the energy industry. AI is changing the way we generate, distribute, and consume energy. It is also having an impact on a wide range of industries, including healthcare, finance, transportation, and criminal justice. As AI becomes more integrated into the energy industry, it is important to understand the impact it is having and to consider how the energy industry can use it to improve efficiency, reduce costs, and promote sustainable energy practices.

Applications of AI in Energy

AI is being used in a wide range of applications in the energy industry, including energy management, predictive maintenance, and renewable energy. In energy management, for example, AI is being used to analyze energy consumption data and optimize energy usage. In predictive maintenance, AI is being used to predict equipment failures and schedule maintenance. In renewable energy, AI is being used to optimize the performance of solar and wind energy systems.

Challenges in AI and Energy

As AI becomes more integrated into the energy industry, there are a number of challenges that need to be addressed. One of the main challenges is ensuring that AI is being used in a way that is fair and just. This includes ensuring that AI systems do not perpetuate or exacerbate existing biases and discrimination. Additionally, there are concerns about the potential for AI to be used in ways that violate privacy and civil liberties. Another challenge is ensuring that energy companies and organizations are able to effectively implement and integrate AI into their work, which can be a significant undertaking.

Tools and Frameworks for AI and Energy

There are various tools and frameworks available for addressing the impact of AI on the energy industry, including the IEEE Global Initiative on Ethics of Autonomous and Intelligent Systems, the AI Ethics Lab, and the AI Ethics Lab at the Oxford Internet Institute. These organizations provide guidelines and best practices for the ethical development and use of AI systems in the energy industry. Additionally, there are also frameworks for evaluating the impact of AI on the energy industry, such as the International Energy Agency's Energy and AI Roadmap, which provides a framework for discussing the impacts of AI on the energy industry and for developing policies to address these impacts.

Case Study:

An example of the impact of AI on the energy industry is the use of AI in energy management. Companies are using AI to analyze energy consumption data and optimize energy usage, which can improve efficiency and reduce costs. However, there are concerns about the potential for AI to perpetuate existing biases and discrimination in energy management. Additionally, there are concerns about the potential for AI to be used in ways that violate privacy and civil liberties of individuals and companies, such as sharing energy consumption data without consent.

References:

- Brynjolfsson, E., & McAfee, A. (2014). The second machine age: work, progress, and prosperity in a time of brilliant technologies. WW Norton & Company.
- Brynjolfsson, E., & McAfee, A. (2017). Machine, platform, crowd: harnessing our digital future. WW Norton & Company.
- Domingos, P. (2015). The master algorithm: how the quest for the ultimate

learning machine will remake our world. Basic books.

- International Energy Agency. (2018). Energy and AI Roadmap. Retrieved from https://www.iea.org/reports/energy-and-ai-roadmap

In conclusion, the field of Artificial Intelligence (AI) is rapidly advancing and it is having a significant impact on the energy industry. AI is changing the way we generate, distribute, and consume energy. As AI becomes more integrated into the energy industry, it is important to understand the impact it is having and to consider how the energy industry can use it to improve efficiency, reduce costs, and promote sustainable energy practices. However, there are challenges in ensuring that AI is being used in a way that is fair and just, and that energy companies and organizations are able to effectively implement and integrate AI into their work. It is important to use the available tools and frameworks for AI and energy to ensure the responsible development and use of AI in the energy industry. Additionally, it is essential to ensure that the privacy rights and civil liberties of individuals and companies are protected and that AI systems do not perpetuate or exacerbate existing biases and discrimination in the energy industry. As the use of AI in the energy industry continues to grow, it is crucial to consider the long-term impacts and to develop policies and regulations that ensure the safe and ethical integration of AI in the energy industry.

Chapter 26: AI and Agriculture

Understanding the Impact of Artificial Intelligence on Agriculture

The field of Artificial Intelligence (AI) is rapidly advancing, and it is having a significant impact on agriculture. AI is changing the way we grow, harvest, and distribute food. It is also having an impact on a wide range of industries, including healthcare, finance, transportation, and criminal justice. As AI becomes more integrated into agriculture, it is important to understand the impact it is having and to consider how agriculture can use it to improve crop yields, reduce costs, and promote sustainable farming practices.

Applications of AI in Agriculture

AI is being used in a wide range of applications in agriculture, including precision farming, crop monitoring, and animal welfare. In precision farming, for example, AI is being used to optimize crop yields by analyzing weather and soil data. In crop monitoring, AI is being used to detect crop diseases and pests. In animal welfare, AI is being used to monitor and optimize the health and well-being of livestock.

Challenges in AI and Agriculture

As AI becomes more integrated into agriculture, there are a number of challenges that need to be addressed. One of the main challenges is ensuring that AI is being used in a way that is fair and just. This includes ensuring that AI systems do not perpetuate or exacerbate existing biases and discrimination. Additionally, there are concerns about the potential for AI to be used in ways that violate privacy and civil liberties. Another challenge is ensuring that farmers and agricultural organizations are able to effectively implement and integrate AI into their work, which can be a significant undertaking.

Tools and Frameworks for AI and Agriculture

There are various tools and frameworks available for addressing the impact of AI on agriculture, including the IEEE Global Initiative on Ethics of Autonomous and Intelligent Systems, the AI Ethics Lab, and the AI Ethics Lab at the Oxford Internet Institute. These organizations provide guidelines and best practices for the ethical development and use of AI systems in agriculture. Additionally, there are also frameworks for evaluating the impact of AI on agriculture, such as the FAO's AI in Agriculture Roadmap, which provides a framework for discussing the impacts of AI on agriculture and for developing policies to address these impacts.

Case Study:

An example of the impact of AI on agriculture is the use of AI in precision farming. Companies are using AI to optimize crop yields by analyzing weather and soil data, which can improve crop yields and reduce costs. However, there are concerns about the potential for AI to perpetuate existing biases and discrimination in precision farming. Additionally, there are concerns about the potential for AI to be used in ways that violate privacy and civil liberties of farmers, such as sharing farming data without consent.

References:

- Brynjolfsson, E., & McAfee, A. (2014). The second machine age: work, progress, and prosperity in a time of brilliant technologies. WW Norton & Company.
- Brynjolfsson, E., & McAfee, A. (2017). Machine, platform, crowd: harnessing our digital future. WW Norton & Company.
- Domingos, P. (2015). The master algorithm: how the quest for the ultimate

learning machine will remake our world. Basic books.

- FAO. (2019). AI in Agriculture Roadmap. Retrieved from http://www.fao.org/ai-in-agriculture-road map/en/

In conclusion, the field of Artificial Intelligence (AI) is rapidly advancing and it is having a significant impact on agriculture. AI is changing the way we grow, harvest, and distribute food. As AI becomes more integrated into agriculture, it is important to understand the impact it is having and to consider how agriculture can use it to improve crop yields, reduce costs, and promote sustainable farming practices. However, there are challenges in ensuring that AI is being used in a way that is fair and just, and that farmers and agricultural organizations are able to effectively implement and integrate AI into their work. It is important to use the available tools and frameworks for AI and agriculture to ensure the responsible development and use of AI in agriculture. Additionally, it is essential to ensure that the privacy rights and civil liberties of farmers are protected and that AI systems do not perpetuate or exacerbate existing biases and discrimination in agriculture. As the use of AI in agriculture continues to grow, it is crucial to consider the long-term impacts and to develop policies and regulations that ensure the safe and ethical integration of AI in agriculture.

Chapter 27: AI and Environment

Understanding the Impact of Artificial Intelligence on the Environment

The field of Artificial Intelligence (AI) is rapidly advancing, and it is having a significant impact on the environment. AI is changing the way we monitor, manage, and protect natural resources. It is also having an impact on a wide range of industries, including healthcare, finance, transportation, and criminal justice. As AI becomes more integrated into environmental management, it is important to understand the impact it is having and to consider how AI can be used to improve sustainability, reduce pollution, and protect biodiversity.

Applications of AI in Environment

AI is being used in a wide range of applications in environmental management, including natural resource management, waste management, and conservation. In natural resource management, for example, AI is being used to optimize water and energy usage. In waste management, AI is being used to optimize recycling and composting. In conservation, AI is being used to monitor wildlife populations and detect illegal poaching.

Challenges in AI and Environment

As AI becomes more integrated into environmental management, there are a number of challenges that need to be addressed. One of the main challenges is ensuring that AI is being used in a way that is fair and just. This includes ensuring that AI systems do not perpetuate or exacerbate existing biases and discrimination. Additionally, there are concerns about the potential for AI to be used in ways that violate privacy and civil liberties. Another challenge is ensuring that environmental organizations and agencies are able to effectively implement and integrate AI into their work, which can be a significant undertaking.

Tools and Frameworks for AI and Environment

There are various tools and frameworks available for addressing the impact of AI on the environment, including the IEEE Global Initiative on Ethics of Autonomous and Intelligent Systems, the AI Ethics Lab, and the AI Ethics Lab at the Oxford Internet Institute. These organizations provide guidelines and best practices for the ethical development and use of AI systems in environmental management. Additionally, there are also frameworks for evaluating the impact of AI on the environment, such as the UN Environment Programme's AI for the Environment initiative, which provides a framework for discussing the impacts of AI on the environment and for developing policies to address these impacts.

Case Study:

An example of the impact of AI on the environment is the use of AI in natural resource management. Companies are using AI to optimize water and energy usage, which can improve sustainability and reduce pollution. However, there are concerns about the potential for AI to perpetuate existing biases and discrimination in natural resource management. Additionally, there are concerns about the potential for AI to be used in ways that violate privacy and civil liberties of individuals and organizations, such as sharing environmental data without consent.

References:

- Brynjolfsson, E., & McAfee, A. (2014). The second machine age: work, progress, and prosperity in a time of brilliant technologies. WW Norton & Company.
- Brynjolfsson, E., & McAfee, (2017). Machine, platform, crowd: harnessing

our digital future. WW Norton & Company.

- Domingos, P. (2015). The master algorithm: how the quest for the ultimate learning machine will remake our world. Basic books.
- UN Environment Programme. (2019). AI for the Environment. Retrieved from https://www.unenvironment.org/explore-topics/artificial-intelligence/what-we-do/ai-environment

In conclusion, the field of Artificial Intelligence (AI) is rapidly advancing and it is having a significant impact on the environment. AI is changing the way we monitor, manage, and protect natural resources. As AI becomes more integrated into environmental management, it is important to understand the impact it is having and to consider how AI can be used to improve sustainability, reduce pollution, and protect biodiversity. However, there are challenges in ensuring that AI is being used in a way that is fair and just, and that environmental organizations and agencies are able to effectively implement and integrate AI into their work. It is important to use the available tools and frameworks for AI and the environment to ensure the responsible development and use of AI in environmental management. Additionally, it is essential to ensure that the privacy rights and civil liberties of individuals and organizations are protected and that AI systems do not perpetuate or exacerbate existing biases and discrimination in environmental management. As the use of AI in environmental management continues to grow, it is crucial to consider the long-term impacts and to develop policies and regulations that ensure the safe and ethical integration of AI in environmental management.

Chapter 28: AI and Space

Understanding the Impact of Artificial Intelligence on Space Exploration

The field of Artificial Intelligence (AI) is rapidly advancing, and it is having a significant impact on space exploration. AI is changing the way we design, operate, and analyze data from space missions. It is also having an impact on a wide range of industries, including healthcare, finance, transportation, and criminal justice. As

AI becomes more integrated into space exploration, it is important to understand the impact it is having and to consider how AI can be used to improve the efficiency, safety, and scientific returns of space missions.

Applications of AI in Space

AI is being used in a wide range of applications in space exploration, including spacecraft design, autonomous navigation, and data analysis. In spacecraft design, for example, AI is being used to optimize the performance of propulsion systems. In autonomous navigation, AI is being used to control the flight path of spacecraft. In data analysis, AI is being used to extract valuable information from images and sensor data.

Challenges in AI and Space

As AI becomes more integrated into space exploration, there are a number of challenges that need to be addressed. One of the main challenges is ensuring that AI is being used in a way that is safe and reliable. This includes ensuring that AI systems do not malfunction or make dangerous decisions. Additionally, there are concerns about the potential for AI to be used in ways that violate privacy and civil liberties. Another challenge is ensuring that space agencies and organizations are able to effectively implement and integrate AI into their work, which can be a significant undertaking.

Tools and Frameworks for AI and Space

There are various tools and frameworks available for addressing the impact of AI on space exploration, including the IEEE Global Initiative on Ethics of Autonomous and Intelligent Systems, the AI Ethics Lab, and the AI Ethics Lab at the Oxford Internet Institute. These organizations provide guidelines and best practices for the ethical development and use of AI systems in space exploration. Additionally, there are also frameworks for evaluating the impact of AI on space exploration, such as the International Space Station's AI for Space initiative, which provides a framework for discussing the impacts of AI on space exploration and for developing policies to address these impacts.

Case Study:

An example of the impact of AI on space exploration is the use of AI in autonomous navigation. Companies are using AI to control the flight path of spacecraft, which can improve the efficiency and safety of space missions. However, there are concerns about the potential for AI to malfunction or make dangerous decisions. Additionally, there are concerns about the potential for AI to be used in ways that violate privacy and civil liberties of individuals and organizations, such as collecting and sharing data without consent.

References:

- Brynjolfsson, E., & McAfee, A. (2014). The second machine age: work, progress, and prosperity in a time of brilliant technologies. WW Norton & Company.
- Brynjolfsson, E., & McAfee, A. (2017). Machine, platform, crowd: harnessing our digital future. WW Norton & Company.

- Domingos, P. (2015). The master algorithm: how the quest for the ultimate learning machine will remake our world. Basic books.
- International Space Station. (2019). AI for Space. Retrieved from https://www.iss.org/ai-for-space

In conclusion, the field of Artificial Intelligence (AI) is rapidly advancing and it is having a significant impact on space exploration. AI is changing the way we design, operate, and analyze data from space missions. As AI becomes more integrated into space exploration, it is important to understand the impact it is having and to consider how AI can be used to improve the efficiency, safety, and scientific returns of space missions. However, there are challenges in ensuring that AI is being used in a way that is safe and reliable, and that space agencies and organizations are able to effectively implement and integrate AI into their work. It is important to use the available tools and frameworks for AI and space to ensure the responsible development and use of

AI in space exploration. Additionally, it is essential to ensure that the privacy rights and civil liberties of individuals and organizations are protected and that AI systems do not perpetuate or exacerbate existing biases and discrimination in space exploration. As the use of AI in space exploration continues to grow, it is crucial to consider the long-term impacts and to develop policies and regulations that ensure the safe and ethical integration of AI in space exploration.

Chapter 29: AI and Military

Understanding the Impact of Artificial Intelligence on Military Operations

The field of Artificial Intelligence (AI) is rapidly advancing, and it is having a significant impact on military operations. AI is changing the way we plan, execute, and evaluate military operations. It is also having an impact on a wide range of industries, including healthcare, finance, transportation, and criminal justice. As AI becomes more integrated into military operations, it is important to understand the impact it is having and to consider how AI can be used to improve the efficiency, effectiveness, and safety of military operations.

Applications of AI in Military

AI is being used in a wide range of applications in military operations, including planning, execution, and evaluation. In planning, for example, AI is being used to optimize the allocation of resources and to predict potential threats. In execution, AI is being used to control autonomous weapons and to analyze sensor data. In evaluation, AI is being used to analyze the effectiveness of military operations and to detect patterns in battlefield data.

Challenges in AI and Military

As AI becomes more integrated into military operations, there are a number of challenges that need to be addressed. One of the main challenges is ensuring that AI is being used in a way that is safe and reliable. This includes ensuring that AI systems do not malfunction or make dangerous decisions. Additionally, there are concerns about the potential for AI to be used in ways that violate privacy and civil liberties. Another challenge is ensuring that military organizations and agencies are able to effectively implement and integrate AI into their work, which can be a significant undertaking.

Tools and Frameworks for AI and Military

There are various tools and frameworks available for addressing the impact of AI on military operations, including the IEEE Global Initiative on Ethics of Autonomous and Intelligent Systems, the AI Ethics Lab, and the AI Ethics Lab at the Oxford Internet Institute. These organizations provide guidelines and best practices for the ethical development and use of AI systems in military operations. Additionally, there are also frameworks for evaluating the impact of AI on military operations, such as the Joint AI Center's AI Ethics Framework, which provides a framework for discussing the impacts of AI on military operations and for developing policies to address these impacts.

Case Study:

An example of the impact of AI on military operations is the use of AI in autonomous weapons. Companies are using AI to control the flight path and decision making of autonomous weapons, which can improve the efficiency and safety of military operations. However, there are concerns about the potential for AI to malfunction or make dangerous decisions. Additionally, there are concerns about the potential for AI to be used in ways that violate privacy and civil liberties of individuals and organizations, such as collecting and sharing sensitive information without consent.

References:

- Brynjolfsson, E., & McAfee, A. (2014). The second machine age: work, progress, and prosperity in a time of brilliant technologies. WW Norton & Company.
- Brynjolfsson, E., & McAfee, A. (2017). Machine, platform, crowd: harnessing

our digital future. WW Norton & Company.

- Domingos, P. (2015). The master algorithm: how the quest for the ultimate learning machine will remake our world. Basic books.
- Joint AI Center. (2019). AI Ethics Framework. Retrieved from https://www.jointai.mil/ai-ethics-framework

In conclusion, the field of Artificial Intelligence (AI) is rapidly advancing and it is having a significant impact on military operations. AI is changing the way we plan, execute, and evaluate military operations. As AI becomes more integrated into military operations, it is important to understand the impact it is having and to consider how AI can be used to improve the efficiency, effectiveness, and safety of military operations. However, there are challenges in ensuring that AI is being used in a way that is safe and reliable, and that military organizations and agencies are able to effectively implement and integrate AI into their work. It is important to use the available tools and frameworks for AI and military to ensure the responsible development and use of AI in military operations. Additionally, it is essential to ensure that the privacy rights and civil liberties of individuals and organizations are protected and that AI systems do not perpetuate or exacerbate existing biases and discrimination in military operations. As the use of AI in military operations continues to grow, it is crucial to consider the long-term impacts and to develop policies and regulations that ensure the safe and ethical integration of AI in military operations.

Chapter 30: AI and Government

Understanding the Impact of Artificial Intelligence on Government Operations

The field of Artificial Intelligence (AI) is rapidly advancing, and it is having a significant impact on government operations. AI is changing the way we plan, execute, and evaluate government policies and programs. It is also having an impact on a wide range of industries, including healthcare, finance, transportation, and criminal justice. As AI becomes more integrated into government operations, it is important to understand the impact it is having and to consider how AI can be used to improve the efficiency, effectiveness, and fairness of government operations.

Applications of AI in Government

AI is being used in a wide range of applications in government operations, including policy planning, program execution, and evaluation. In policy planning, for example, AI is being used to analyze data and predict potential outcomes of different policy options. In program execution, AI is being used to automate administrative tasks and to analyze data from government programs. In evaluation, AI is being used to analyze the effectiveness of government policies and programs and to detect patterns in government data.

Challenges in AI and Government

As AI becomes more integrated into government operations, there are a number of challenges that need to be addressed. One of the main challenges is ensuring that AI is being used in a way that is fair and just. This includes ensuring that AI systems do not perpetuate or exacerbate existing biases and discrimination. Additionally, there are concerns about the potential for AI to be used in ways that violate privacy and civil liberties. Another challenge is ensuring that government organizations and agencies are able to effectively implement and integrate AI into their work, which can be a significant undertaking.

Tools and Frameworks for AI and Government

There are various tools and frameworks available for addressing the impact of AI on government operations, including the IEEE Global Initiative on Ethics of Autonomous and Intelligent Systems, the AI Ethics Lab, and the AI Ethics Lab at the Oxford Internet Institute. These organizations provide guidelines and best practices for the ethical development and use of

AI systems in government operations. Additionally, there are also frameworks for evaluating the impact of AI on government operations, such as the AI for Government initiative, which provides a framework for discussing the impacts of AI on government operations and for developing policies to address these impacts.

Case Study:

An example of the impact of AI on government operations is the use of AI in automating administrative tasks such as processing applications for government services and benefits. Companies are using AI to automate these tasks, which can improve the efficiency and accuracy of government operations. However, there are concerns about the potential for AI to perpetuate or exacerbate existing biases and discrimination, particularly in cases where AI systems are trained on biased data. Additionally, there are concerns about the potential for AI to be used in ways that violate privacy and civil liberties of individuals and organizations, such as collecting and sharing sensitive information without consent.

References:

- Brynjolfsson, E., & McAfee, A. (2014). The second machine age: work, progress, and prosperity in a time of brilliant technologies. WW Norton & Company.
- Brynjolfsson, E., & McAfee, A. (2017). Machine, platform, crowd: harnessing our digital future. WW Norton & Company.
- Domingos, P. (2015). The master algorithm: how the quest for the ultimate learning machine will remake our world. Basic books.
- AI for Government. (2019). AI for Government. Retrieved from https://www.aiforgov.com/

In conclusion, the field of Artificial Intelligence (AI) is rapidly advancing and it is having a significant impact on government operations. AI is changing the way we plan, execute, and evaluate government policies and programs. As AI becomes more integrated into government operations, it is important to understand the impact it is having and to consider how AI can be used to improve the efficiency, effectiveness, and fairness of government operations. However, there are challenges in ensuring that AI is being used in a way that is fair and just, and that government organizations and agencies are able to effectively implement and integrate AI into their work. It is important to use the available tools and frameworks for AI and government to ensure the responsible development and use of AI in government operations. Additionally, it is essential to ensure that the privacy rights and civil liberties of individuals and organizations are protected and that AI systems do not perpetuate or exacerbate existing biases and discrimination in government operations. As the use of AI in government operations continues to grow, it is crucial to consider the long-term impacts and to develop policies and regulations that ensure the safe and ethical integration of AI in government operations.

Chapter 31: Conclusion

Artificial Intelligence (AI) is rapidly advancing and it is having a significant impact on our world. From healthcare to finance, transportation to criminal justice, and many more, AI is changing the way we live and work. As AI becomes more integrated into our lives, it is important to understand the impact it is having and to consider how AI can be used to improve our world.

In this book, we have explored the various aspects of AI, including its history, types, and applications. We have also discussed the challenges and ethical considerations associated with AI, and the tools and frameworks available for addressing these issues. We have looked at the impact of AI on various industries and sectors, including healthcare, finance, transportation, criminal justice, and more.

One of the main challenges associated with AI is ensuring that it is used in a way that is safe and reliable. This includes ensuring that AI systems do not malfunction or make dangerous decisions. Additionally, there are concerns about the potential for AI to be used in ways that violate privacy and civil liberties. Another challenge is ensuring that organizations and agencies are able to effectively implement and integrate AI into their work, which can be a significant undertaking.

To address these challenges, we have looked at various tools and frameworks available for addressing the impact of AI on different industries and sectors. These include the IEEE Global Initiative on Ethics of Autonomous and

Intelligent Systems, the AI Ethics Lab, and the AI Ethics Lab at the Oxford Internet Institute. These organizations provide guidelines and best practices for the ethical development and use of AI systems. Additionally, there are also frameworks for evaluating the impact of AI on different industries and sectors, such as the AI for Government initiative and the Joint AI Center's AI Ethics Framework.

In conclusion, AI is rapidly advancing and it is having a significant impact on our world. As AI becomes more integrated into our lives, it is important to understand the impact it is having and to consider how AI can be used to improve our world. However, there are challenges associated with AI and it is essential to ensure that it is used in a way that is safe, reliable, and ethical. By understanding the impact of AI, its challenges and ethical considerations, and the tools and frameworks available for addressing these issues, we can ensure the responsible development and use of AI in our world.

Printed in Great Britain
by Amazon